Teaching With Dear Canada

Build Important Social Studies and Language Skills with Historical Fiction

by

Amy von Heyking

SCHOLASTIC Teaching Resources

Scholastic Canada Ltd.

Table of Contents

Teaching Social Studies with Historical Fiction 3

A Timeline of Canadian History 6

Alone in an Untamed Land: The *Filles du Roi* Diary of Hélène St. Onge
Summary/What's Going On in the World in 1666? 9
Prior Knowledge/Discussion Questions 10
Extended Activities 14
Reproducibles 15
Bibliography 17

Whispers of War: The War of 1812 Diary of Susanna Merritt
Summary/What's Going On in the World in 1812? 18
Prior Knowledge/Discussion Questions 19
Extended Activities 23
Reproducibles 24
Bibliography 26

A Ribbon of Shining Steel: The Railway Diary of Kate Cameron
Summary/What's Going On in the World in 1882? 27
Prior Knowledge/Discussion Questions 28
Extended Activities 31
Reproducibles 32
Bibliography 34

Brothers Far from Home: The World War I Diary of Eliza Bates
Summary/What's Going On in the World in 1916?..35
Prior Knowledge/Discussion Questions 36
Extended Activities 41
Reproducibles 42
Bibliography 44

Activities for General Use 45

Teaching Social Studies with Historical Fiction

Historical fiction can be a wonderful way to capture students' interest in the study of the past. It can, however, be used for more than just an introduction to a history unit.

What Can Literature Do for Social Studies Instruction?

1. By including historical fiction in social studies, teachers can provide a greater variety of books for children. This simply makes sense since we know that not all the children in our classrooms are reading at the same level (McGowan and Guzzetti 1991).
2. The teaching of history includes bringing children to an understanding of many complex concepts: change, community, tradition and class, to name a few. Many writers have recognized that stories clarify these concepts for children because they personalize them: they provide a relevant and meaningful context that children can identify with (McGowan and Guzzetti 1991; Van Middendorp and Lee 1994; Brozo and Tomlinson 1986). The authors of historical fiction use language and images evocatively to transport children into different times and places. A 1992 study by Guzzetti, Kowalinski and McGowan demonstrated that sixth-grade students actually learned more social studies concepts and seemed to have a greater understanding of those concepts when they were taught through a literature-based rather than textbook-based approach. Studies have also found that elementary school students' interest in history and their retention of historical information increased when their history instruction included children's literature (Levstik 1986; VanSledright 1995).
3. Reading stories can heighten children's emotional sensitivity. Their moral and social awareness grows when they consider reasons for people's behaviour in other times, other places or specific situations. Most children have not had sufficient life experience to imagine, let alone identify with, others. Stories provide the "insider's perspective" that allows children to connect with people in other times and places and come to a deeper understanding of others' experiences.

Cautions and Guidelines

Some important cautions or concerns have been raised about the use of historical fiction in social studies instruction.

1. Roberta McKay reminds us that literature is written to tell a story, not to convey information or clarify concepts. Teaching social studies content through literature can distort the purpose of the story. It should not be used as a substitute for the textbook (McKay 1995). When using historical fiction like the Dear Canada diaries, give children a chance to respond aesthetically to the stories they read or listen to. Do not jump into social studies questions or activities without giving children a chance to appreciate and discuss the important literary elements of the diaries. Talk about the way the authors used language in the diaries. (Examples:

How does the language or vocabulary the authors used make it seem as if they really were written long ago? Make a glossary of all the unusual or new words. How did they evoke a sense of the past? What were the important turning points in the diary? How did the authors make you want to keep reading? Did you get a real sense of place in the description of the setting? Discuss the characters in the diaries. Would you like to meet the fictional writer of the diary? Would she be a good friend?)

2. It is vital that even the youngest students begin to distinguish between factual and fictional writing. Integrating fictional stories into lessons in a content area (which is usually factual) can confuse them if explicit instruction in the two kinds of writing is not given. Teachers must teach the distinction between fiction and non-fiction literature explicitly, directly and often. Indeed, Levstik and Barton suggest that historical narratives carry extraordinary authority for children, and reading them to begin a unit may actually undermine children's attempts to do research on the topic or approach their research in an objective way. It takes careful, deliberate and teacher-directed work with fiction and non-fiction text to help children understand the complex "truth" of an historical episode (2001). Reading a range of fiction and non-fiction books on the same subject will help children examine various books critically, determining the interpretation the authors present. Levstik (1993) tells us that children "need to be exposed not just to textbooks and historical fiction, but also to biographies, autobiographies, informational texts, and even oral history; they need to be able to distinguish the features of each form and to recognize their strengths and limitations. They will then learn to ask who is telling the story and to whom, and who is left out." Consider asking students how the authors of the Dear Canada diaries make their characters seem like "real" people. As students are reading, continually ask them how the author might have known specific historical details. (For example: How would Maxine Trottier know that people in New France ate muskrat? How did Julie Lawson know what kinds of things children would have been reading in their school texts in the 1880s?) After reading the diaries and doing research on the historical period, ask them to identify elements in the diary that are obvious fiction. Use a Venn diagram to compare and contrast the diary with a non-fiction book on the same historical period. Place all the books students consulted on a continuum from "completely fictional" to "completely factual" and ask them to defend the way they placed the books.

3. Using historical fiction can obscure the fact that the past is a different place. While it can be important to motivate students' interest in the past, historical fiction can distort history and the experience of people in the past when it pretends that they were just like us. Anne Scott MacLeod reminds us that "people of the past were not just us in odd clothing. They were people who saw the world differently; approached human relationships differently; people for whom night and day, heat and cold, seasons and work and play had meanings lost to an industrialized world." (Quoted in Edinger 2000, 124.) There is a concern that we are actually encouraging a dangerous "presentism" or "present-mindedness" in children when we

emphasize the similarities between the past and present and suggest to children that they are even capable of understanding the experience of people in the past through the reading of historical fiction. Remember to ask students critical questions about the Dear Canada diaries when you are reading them: Why are real diaries written by children so difficult to find? Is it realistic to imagine girls like these keeping diaries? Why are all the fictional writers of the diaries a little bit eccentric? In what ways are the girls written to appeal to modern readers?

These cautions and guidelines are intended not to discourage teachers from using historical fiction, but are simply a reminder that it should be used judiciously and appropriately. At its most powerful, historical fiction becomes a springboard for students' own questions about the past.

Activities for General Use

Three activities that can be applied to any of the Dear Canada books are available on pages 45 to 47. (Activities and reproducibles for use with specific titles are included within each title's section.)

Bibliography

Brophy, Jere and VanSledright, Bruce. (1997). *Teaching and Learning History in Elementary Schools.* New York: Teachers College Press.

Brozo, W.G. and Tomlinson, C.M. (1986). "Literature: The Key to Lively Content Courses." *The Reading Teacher,* 40, 3: 288–93.

Davis, John C., III and Palmer, Jesse. (1992). "A Strategy for Using Children's Literature to Extend the Social Studies Curriculum." *The Social Studies*, 83, 3: 125–128.

Edinger, Monica. (2000). *Seeking History: Teaching with Primary Sources in Grades 4–6.* Portsmouth, N.H.: Heinemann.

Guzzetti, B., Kowalinksi, B. and McGowan, T. (1992). "Using a Literature-Based Approach to Teaching Social Studies." *Journal of Reading*, 36: 114–22.

Jorgensen, Karen L. (1993). *History Workshop: Reconstructing the Past with Elementary Students.* Portsmouth, N.H.: Heinemann.

Levstik, Linda S. (1993). "Making the Past Come to Life." In Bernice E. Cullinan (Ed.), *Fact and Fiction: Literature Across the Curriculum* (pp. 5–13). Newark, DE: International Reading Association.

Levstik, Linda S. (1986). "The Relationship Between Historical Response and Narrative in a Sixth Grade Classroom." *Theory and Research in Social Education,* 14: 1–19.

Levstik, Linda S. and Barton, Keith C. (2001). *Doing History,* 2nd ed. Mahwah, N.J.: Lawrence Erlbaum Associates.

McGowan, T. and Guzzetti, B. (1991). "Promoting Social Studies Understanding Through Literature-Based Instruction." *The Social Studies*, 82, 1: 16–21.

McKay, Roberta. (1997). "Promoting the Aesthetic Experience: Responding to Literature in Social Studies." In Roland Case and Penney Clark (Eds.), *The Canadian Anthology of Social Studies* (pp. 349–360). Vancouver: Pacific Educational Press.

McKay, Roberta. (1995). "Using Literature in Social Studies: A Caution." *Canadian Social Studies,* 29 (3): 95–6.

A Timeline of Canadian History

About 18000 B.C.	The first inhabitants of North America probably cross from Siberia via a land bridge.
About A.D. 1001	Leif Ericsson makes his first voyage to Vinland.
1497	John Cabot makes the first of two voyages for England to the fishing grounds of Newfoundland.
1534	Jacques Cartier claims the Gaspé peninsula for France. The following year he travels up the St. Lawrence to Stadacona (now Québec City) and Hochelaga (now Montréal) and names the territory "Canada."
1576	Martin Frobisher makes the first of three journeys to find the Northwest Passage.
1583	Sir Humphrey Gilbert claims Newfoundland for England.
1604	Samuel de Champlain establishes a colony at Nova Scotia.
1608	Champlain establishes a permanent French colony at Québec.
1615	The first Roman Catholic missionaries attempt to convert aboriginal people to Christianity.
1642	The founding of Montréal.
1649	The Iroquois complete the destruction of the Huron nation and begin to raid French settlements.
1663	Jean Talon is appointed Intendant of New France. King Louis XIV commits to defending the colony and promoting settlement.
1666	***Alone in an Untamed Land***
1670	The British crown grants a charter to the Hudson's Bay Company.
1713	The Treaty of Utrecht.
1749	The British establish Halifax.
1755	The British begin the expulsion of the Acadians.
1756–1763	The Seven Years War between Britain and France, during which the British capture Louisbourg (1758) and Québec in the battle of the Plains of Abraham (1759), and the French surrender New France to the British (1760).
1769	Prince Edward Island becomes a colony of Great Britain.
1774	The passage of the Québec Act.
1776	The creation of the North West Company.
1778	Captain James Cook explores the Pacific Coast.
1775–1783	The American Revolutionary War, during which the Thirteen Colonies gain independence from Great Britain. The people of Québec, Nova Scotia and Prince Edward Island remain loyal to Great Britain. About forty thousand Loyalists from the Thirteen Colonies join them.

1791	Québec is divided into two separate colonies: Lower and Upper Canada.
1792	Captain George Vancouver makes the first of three voyages to explore Vancouver Island and the coast of British Columbia.
1793	Explorer Alexander Mackenzie crosses the Rocky and Coastal Mountains to reach the Pacific Ocean.
1793	John Graves Simcoe establishes York (now Toronto) on the shore of Lake Ontario.
1811	The first group of Lord Selkirk's settlers arrives at Hudson Bay.
1812	***Whispers of War***
1812–1815	The War of 1812, between Great Britain and the United States, in which Isaac Brock is killed (Battle of Queenston Heights in 1812), Laura Secord becomes a hero (1813) and Tecumseh dies (1813).
1837	Rebellions in Upper and Lower Canada result in a visit from Lord Durham and the recommendation that the colonies should receive responsible government.
1841	The Act of Union unites Upper and Lower Canada into the Province of Canada.
1843	Victoria is established on Vancouver Island.
1851	Canada's first postage stamp is issued. It has only been possible to send mail overseas for about ten years.
1857	Ottawa becomes the new capital of Canada.
1858	British Columbia becomes a colony of Great Britain when gold is discovered in the Fraser River.
1867	The British North America Act is passed. New Brunswick, Nova Scotia, Québec and Ontario form the Dominion of Canada.
1869	The Métis in the Red River region rebel when Canada purchases the territory from the Hudson's Bay Company.
1870	The province of Manitoba joins Confederation. The Northwest Territories are created.
1871	British Columbia joins Confederation.
1873	The Cypress Hills massacre results in the creation of the North West Mounted Police to keep order in the new territories.
1873	Prince Edward Island joins Confederation.
1882	***A Ribbon of Shining Steel***
1885	The Métis of the Northwest Territories rebel against the Canadian government. Their leader, Louis Riel, is later hanged.

1885	The last spike of the main line of the Canadian Pacific Railway is driven at Craigellachie, British Columbia.
1896	Gold is discovered in the Klondike.
1898	Yukon becomes a federal territory.
1899–1902	Canadians fight for the British during the Boer War in South Africa.
1905	Saskatchewan and Alberta join Confederation.
1914–1918	Britain declares war on Germany. Canada participates as part of the British Empire.
1916–1918	***Brothers Far from Home***
1917	The Halifax explosion.
1918	Women are granted the right to vote in federal elections.
1919	The Winnipeg general strike.
1927	The first coast-to-coast radio broadcast in Canada.
1929	The Persons Case.
1929	The stock market crash of October 29 marks the beginning of the Great Depression.
1936	The establishment of the Canadian Broadcasting Corporation.
1939–45	Canada participates in the Second World War.
1947	The oil strike at Leduc No. 1 in Alberta marks the beginning of the province's oil boom.
1949	Newfoundland joins Confederation.
1960	Aboriginal people living on reserves are granted the right to vote in federal elections.
1965	Canada adopts a new flag featuring a red maple leaf.
1970	The FLQ, a terrorist group attempting to establish an independent Québec through revolution, kidnaps a British trade commissioner and a Québec cabinet minister. The federal government, under Prime Minister Pierre Trudeau, invokes the War Measures Act.
1982	The Constitution Act is passed, along with the Canadian Charter of Rights and Freedoms.
1989	The North American Free Trade Agreement comes into effect.
1999	Nunavut becomes a federal territory.

Alone in an Untamed Land

The *Filles du Roi* Diary of Hélène St. Onge

Montréal, New France, 1666

by Maxine Trottier

Summary: Hélène St. Onge has just lost her father when she and her older sister Catherine learn that they have lost their fortune as well. Relatives convince Catherine to travel to New France where she will eventually become a *fille à marier*, a marriageable woman with a dowry from the King of France himself. She will be expected to marry a man of her choosing in the colony. Hélène accompanies her sister on the voyage across the Atlantic. While the journey is often frightening, Hélène copes with her loneliness by befriending a young girl of mixed French and Mohawk blood, Kateri, and her father, Jean Aubry, a gunsmith returning to his home in Montréal. When Catherine dies on the journey, Hélène takes her place as a *fille à marier*.

In Montréal, Hélène is taken in by her Tante Barbe, who owns an inn. There she learns about life in the colony, its hard work, its dangers, but also its joys. Over the course of a winter she grows and matures until finally she is ready to make her choice of a husband in this new world.

What's Going On in the World in 1666?

- Molière's plays are performed at the French court.
- France captures the islands of Antigua, Montserrat and St. Christopher.
- The English writer John Milton begins *Paradise Lost*.
- Isaac Newton measures the moon's orbit.
- Puritans from Connecticut establish Newark, New Jersey.
- Much of London, England, is destroyed in the Great Fire.
- The first cheddar cheese is made.

Prior Knowledge

Before reading the diary, ensure that students have some background information about the settlement of New France. They should understand the challenges that the French Crown faced in encouraging settlers to cross the ocean, and the risks the *filles à marier* were taking in making the journey and starting a new life in the colony. They should consider why this episode in Canadian history is significant enough to warrant writing about. The diary will be more meaningful if students have some understanding of the role of Roman Catholicism in the lives of settlers and of the religious calendar, particularly the saints' days, to which Hélène often refers. Students should also have some understanding of relations among the French, the Huron and the Iroquois in this period so they understand the dangers Hélène faces and the attitudes of some of the diary's characters toward Kateri and her family. The sources listed in the bibliography include maps of traditional Iroquois and Huron territory that may be useful to share with students.

Discussion Questions

- Find Reignac on a map of France. Hélène's cousin Pierre Demerse comes from La Rochelle. Find La Rochelle on a map. Why would many immigrants to New France have come from this region of France?
- Is Hélène's family wealthy? How do you know (p. 9)?
- Why does cousin Pierre suggest that Hélène and Catherine become nuns (p. 10)?
- Draw Hélène's family tree based on the information you have so far (p. 12).
- Who are *les filles à marier*? What role did they play in the growth of the colony of New France (p. 14)?
- Why does the Captain of *Le Chat Blanc* warn the women about open flames on board the ship (p. 25)?
- Sketch the interior of the ship based on Hélène's description (p. 29).
- Why does Catherine refuse to make friends with the other *filles à marier*? Why does she feel that they are "beneath" her (p. 30)?
- Why might the priest be interested in Monsieur Deschamps's beaver hat (p. 31)? Find some pictures of beaver hats and select the one you think would most resemble Monsieur Deschamps's.

- Why might Kateri have her own room on board the ship? Is that unusual (p. 34)?
- Why would it be "inappropriate" for Hélène to speak to Séraphin (p. 35)?
- What disease do you think Catherine and the others might have died from (p. 44)?
- How does Hélène cope with the loss of her sister? What do you think is going to happen to her now?
- The women on the ship begin to exhibit some of the signs of scurvy (p. 52). Find out more about the disease and its cure. What might happen to them if they don't get to land soon? How might this disease have been prevented?
- Why would Monsieur Aubry be offended by Hélène's gift to Kateri (p. 54)? Make a list of things you now know about him and his character.
- Why would Hélène refuse to attend mass or make confession? Why would this be such a serious offence in the eyes of the *filles à marier*?

Greeting *les filles à marier* at Québec

- Sketch the scene as Hélène's ship approaches Cap Diamant (p. 62). Find pictures of the setting to see how close your sketch might be to what the *filles à marier* would have seen.
- What does Monsieur Aubry mean when he agrees with Hélène that she is not the sort of girl a man looks at twice (pp. 64–65)?
- Why does Hélène agree to become a *fille à marier?* Do you think this is the right decision for her to make?
- Why do all the *filles à marier* dress in their finest clothes for their outing into Québec?
- Why do Monsieur Deschamps and Madame Laurent refuse to let Kateri into the boat when the ship catches fire (p. 72)? Does Hélène do the right thing? Why does she take the action she does?

- Two of the *filles à marier* quickly interview potential husbands and make arrangements to get married in Québec (p. 74). What kinds of questions do they ask the men? Why? Make a list of "The Top Ten Questions *Filles à Marier* Should Ask Before Getting Married."

- Find out more about Marie de l'Incarnation (p. 78). What contributions did she make to the growth of the colony of New France? Do you agree with Hélène that Marie de l'Incarnation was wise to learn aboriginal languages? Why or why not?

First convent of the Ursuline nuns at Québec, built in 1641–42

- Why might Séraphin prefer the life of an *engagé* to the life of a sailor (p. 79)?

- Hélène says that while she first thought Québec a primitive settlement, she now realizes that it is a "bastion of civilization in the wilderness." What does she mean by this (p. 89)? Would Kateri agree?

- Jean tells Hélène that she will face many challenges in New France (p. 90). Take a moment to complete a character sketch of Hélène. Make some predictions about how she might adjust to life in New France. What will she like about the colony? What will be difficult for her?

- When Hélène first sees the Mohawk warriors (p. 91), she is disturbed but senses no danger. Make a quick sketch of the scene, and "quick write" about this meeting from the perspective of one of the Mohawk warriors. How would he describe the French travellers?

- Review the last few diary entries in which Hélène describes Tante Barbe's inn (p. 105). Why might this be a good place for Hélène to live? How will this help her to adjust to life in New France?

- Why does Hélène refuse Monsieur Deschamps's offer of marriage (p. 114)? Would there be any benefits to Hélène marrying him? Why would Hélène be a good choice of wife for Deschamps?

- What do you think Monsieur Aubry wants to discuss with Hélène when he returns (p. 118)?

- Review the descriptions of Tante Barbe's inn. Sketch a floor plan of the inn and a map of the surrounding yard.

- Séraphin helps the soldiers rebuild sections of the palisade around the settlement and says that it is there to offer protection against bears (p. 131). Why is it really there?

- It is clear that Monsieur Aubry wants to marry Hélène someday (p. 150). Create a T-chart and on one side write all the reasons Hélène should marry him. On the other, list reasons she should not.

- Hélène is much younger than Monsieur Aubry, but their age difference was not unusual for couples in New France. Why would women have married so young in those days? Why might men have been older when they married, even for the first time?

- Monsieur Aubry is very close to one community of Mohawks. Why would he give Hélène a pistol to protect herself against others (p. 159)?

- Why doesn't Hélène think a charivari is amusing anymore (p. 180)?

- Why do the Mohawk laughingly wish Jean luck in his marriage to Hélène (p. 186)?

- Hélène ends her diary thinking about the dragonfly as a symbol of life (p. 189). In what ways has she grown and changed in the course of the past year?

- After finishing your reading, discuss whether or not *Alone in an Untamed Land* is an appropriate title for Hélène's diary. Why or why not? If not, create a new title and explain why it is better.

Mohawks at various tasks outside their elm bark lodge

Extended Activities

- As you read or listen to the diary, fill in the reproducible Research Web (p. 15) with information about life in New France.

- Hélène comes from a noble family. Noble families often have crests with symbols that represent the family's history and regional origin. Using the outline on the reproducible (p. 16), create a new family crest for Hélène's and Jean's family, one that reflects their interests, character and experiences in France and New France.

- Write an advertisement for a *fille à marier*. What qualities would a young woman need to successfully adjust to life in New France? What challenges would she face? Think specifically about Hélène's qualities. You might want to complete a character map of Hélène in order to organize your ideas.

- Complete a Venn diagram comparing and contrasting Kateri and Hélène. In what ways are they similar? In what ways are they different? In what ways are they treated differently by others? What do they learn from each other?

- Pretend you are Hélène at the end of the diary. Write the letter to Pierre explaining why you want to stay and make your life in Montréal.

- Pretend that a young girl from her home region in France writes to Hélène and tells her that she is thinking of coming to New France. Write Hélène's reply in which she gives her important advice about becoming a *fille à marier*.

- Find out more about the lives of the men and women who contributed to the colony of New France: Paul de Chomedey de Maisonneuve; Marie de l'Incarnation; Jeanne Mance; Marguerite Bourgeoys; Jean Talon; Bishop Laval; Louis, Comte de Frontenac; Kateri Tekakwitha. Write your report about their accomplishments in the form of a eulogy.

Marguerite Bourgeoys

Name ____

Research Web

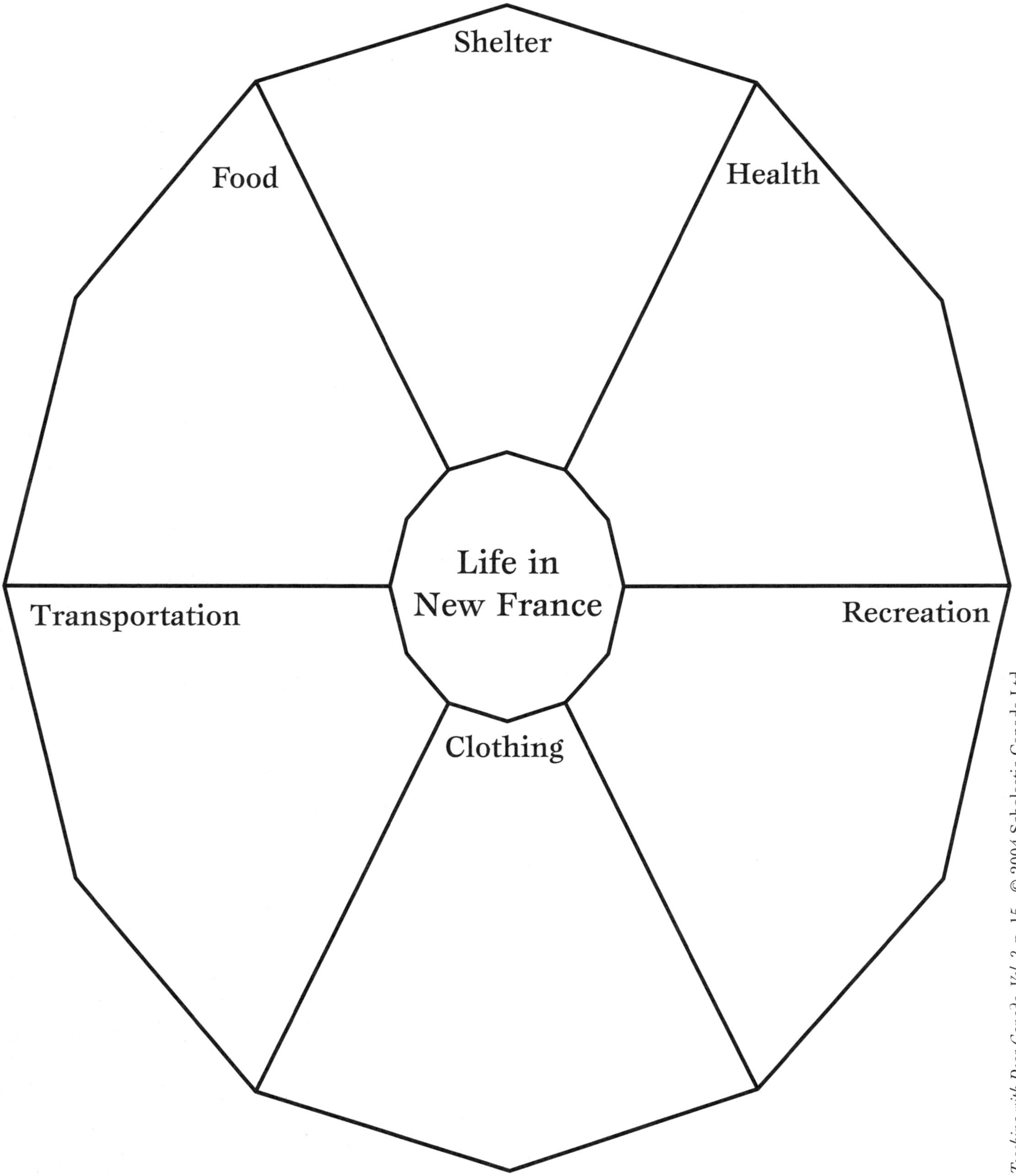

Name ____

Family Crest

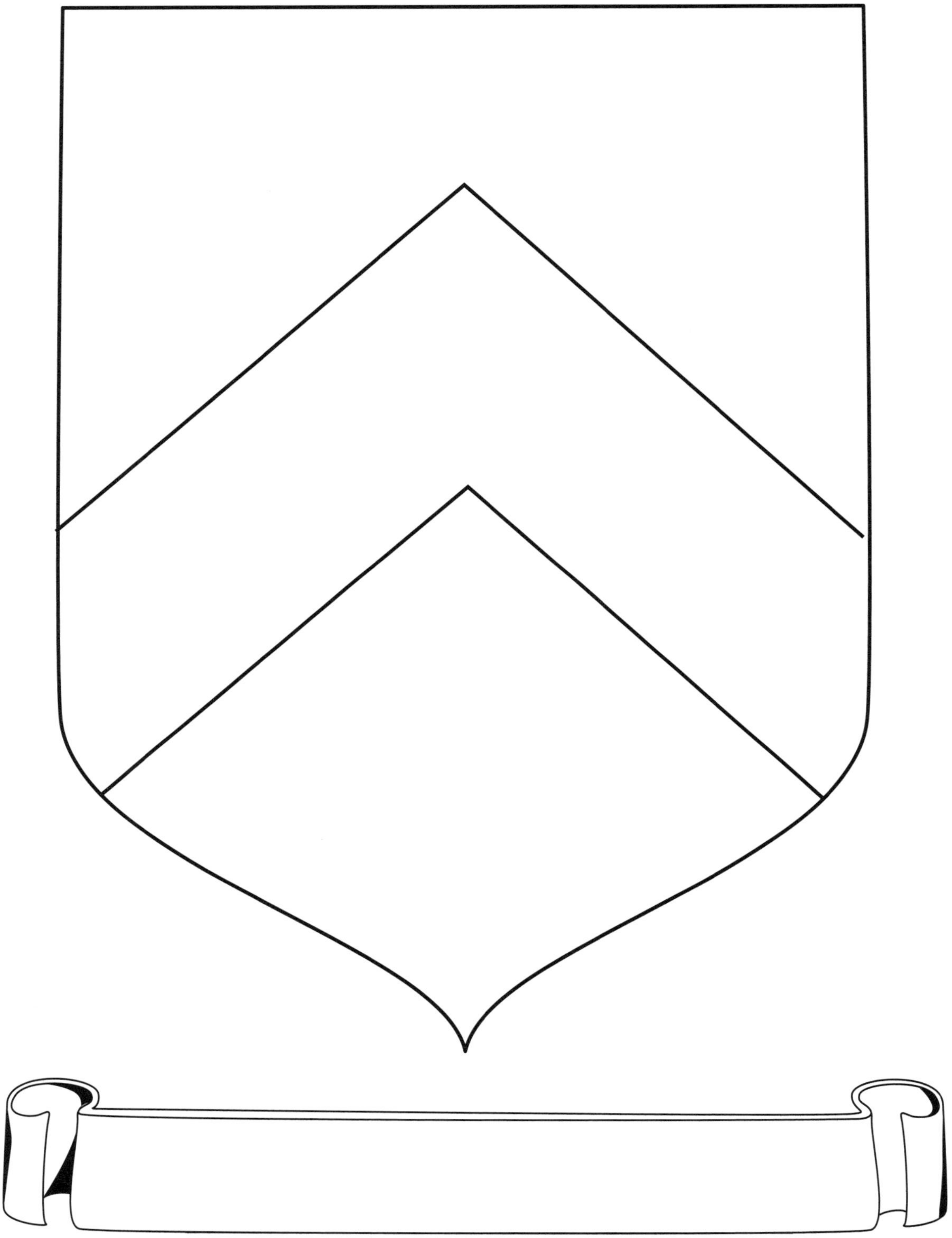

Alone in an Untamed Land

The *Filles du Roi* Diary of Hélène St. Onge

Bibliography

Non-fiction

Baldwin, Douglas. (2003). *New France and the Fur Trade.* Calgary: Weigl Educational Publishers.

Gillis, Jennifer Blizin. (2003). *Life in New France.* Chicago: Heinemann Library.

Hancock, Pat. (1999). *The Penguin Book of Canadian Biography for Young Readers: Early Canada.* Toronto: Penguin Books Canada.

Kalman, Bobbie. (2001). *Life in a Longhouse Village.* St. Catharines: Crabtree Publishing.

Levine, Ellen. (1998). *If You Lived with the Iroquois.* New York: Scholastic Inc.

Livesey, Robert and Smith, A.G. (1990). *New France.* Toronto: Stoddart Kids.

Neering, Rosemary. (1995). *Life in New France.* Markham, ON: Fitzhenry & Whiteside.

Ryan, Marla Felkins and Schmittroth, Linda. (2002). *Mohawk.* San Diego: Blackbirch Press.

Sneve, Virginia Driving Hawk. (1995). *The Iroquois.* New York: Holiday House.

Fiction

Cook, Lyn. (1990). *The Hiding-Place.* Toronto: Key Porter Books.

Metikosh, Anne. (2000). *Terra Incognita.* Vancouver: Ronsdale Press.

Background Information for Teachers

Bumsted, J.M. (2003). *The Peoples of Canada: a Pre-Confederation History,* 2nd ed. Don Mills, ON: Oxford University Press.

Greer, Allan, ed. (2000). *The Jesuit Relations: Natives and Missionaries in Seventeenth-Century North America.* Boston: Bedford/St. Martin's.

Greer, Allan. (1997). *The People of New France.* Toronto: University of Toronto Press.

Moogk, Peter. (2000). *La Nouvelle France: The Making of French Canada, a Cultural History.* East Lansing, MI: Michigan State University Press.

Noel, Janet. (1998). *Women in New France.* Ottawa: Canadian Historical Association.

Websites

http://www.civilization.ca/vmnf/vmnfe.asp
—Virtual Museum of New France

http://collections.ic.gc.ca/premieres_nations/en/
—First Nations of the New France Era

Whispers of War

The War of 1812 Diary of Susanna Merritt

Niagara, Upper Canada, 1812

by Kit Pearson

Summary: Eleven-year-old Susanna Merritt lives on a farm near "the Twelve," or St. Catharines, Upper Canada. It is May, 1812. Great Britain has been at war with France for many years, and now there are rumours that the United States is also going to declare war against Britain. Susanna, like many of her neighbours, is American by background. They are troubled by the prospect of being forced to fight a war against former friends and even relatives. Susanna's father and brother are, however, ready to take up arms when war is finally declared at the end of June. In the months that follow, Susanna meets General Isaac Brock, the commander of British forces in Upper Canada and its Lieutenant-Governor, and she befriends his ward, Ellis. Though not a soldier, she finds herself facing the dangers and confusion of war, and being changed by her experiences.

What's Going On in the World in 1812?

- Napoleon expands his empire across Europe and invades Russia.
- Louisiana becomes a state of the United States.
- Poet Robert Browning and novelist Charles Dickens are born.
- Beethoven composes Symphonies No. 7 and No. 8.
- The population of Lower Canada is 330,000; the population of Upper Canada is 90,000.
- The Red River colony is established at the forks of the Red and Assiniboine Rivers.

Prior Knowledge

Students should have some understanding of the nature of the population of Upper Canada in 1812. They should grasp the difference between the Loyalists who came during the American Revolutionary War, the late Loyalists and the American immigrants who came later, largely for economic reasons. Ask students to predict some difficulties that might have arisen when these people lived close to one another. Review the map on page 215, illustrating the setting of the story, and ensure that students have some understanding of the challenges of pioneer life in this period.

Teachers should provide some background information about Britain's war against Napoleonic France and why the United States sympathized with France. Outline the course and conduct of the war. Students might be struck by the fact that even after the war officially began, the Merritts and other men of the community were occasionally able to come home. The conduct of the war was interrupted by armistices or truces. Some description of the nature of early 19th century warfare might help to explain this.

Discussion Questions

- What does Susanna mean when she says she would rather her life be dull than dangerous (p. 4)?

- Susanna laughs at Hamilton when he buys a new device for cleaning his teeth. How do you think she cleans her teeth?

- Use Susanna's description of "the Twelve" on page 8 to make a quick sketch map of the settlement. Place the Merritts' and the Seabrooks' farms as well as the forest on the map, too.

- In what way is Upper Canada the mouse caught between "the lion," Britain, and "the eagle," the United States (p. 12)? Draw an editorial cartoon that illustrates this dilemma. Choose different images to symbolize each nation if you wish.

- Why will Abbie no longer be able to attend school?

- What differences do you notice between Susanna's schooling and your own?

- Draft a rough copy of Susanna's family tree. Note a few important facts about each person for reference as you read the rest of the diary.

- Susanna and the other children at school create quite a complex game based on the Biblical story of Noah's ark. Why would they spend so much time and effort on a game based on a Bible story?

General Isaac Brock

- Virtually everyone Susanna knows, including her parents and Tabitha, has suffered tragic losses. Why might this be? Do you think the author is realistic in giving these characters such sad stories?

- Why would Hamilton have to "cut" Susanna a pen (p. 30)?

- Why do Susanna and Abbie fight (pp. 32–35)?

- Look on a map to see the distance between "the Twelve" (St. Catharines) and Niagara. Why would it take four hours to make this trip (p. 40)?

- Susanna calls General Brock the "President" of Upper Canada (p. 42). Is this his real title? Why would she call him that?

- Obviously Susanna's father is an important man in Niagara. What evidence have you read to indicate that Susanna's family is privileged or upper class? What evidence have you read that indicates that they do not seem very privileged? How do you account for this?

- Find out more about the troops who marched on the plain near Fort George (p. 47). Susanna saw regular British troops, her father and brother in the uniform of the Niagara Light Dragoons, and her neighbour Mr. Seabrook in regular clothes with the militia. What is the difference between these groups? What responsibilities do they have? If a war comes, who do you think will fight most vigorously to defend Upper Canada? Why?

- Susanna obviously enjoys her first visit to Niagara Falls. Create a postcard that Susanna might send to Tabitha, briefly describing her impressions of the Falls.

View of Queenston from Queenston Heights, 1816-17

- Why does Maria want to visit the Secords (p. 56)? Why does her mother refuse her request?

- Which do you think would be better: living in Niagara or at "the Twelve"? Why?

- Why does Mr. Simmons return to the United States? Does Mr. Seabrook agree with Mr. Simmons? Hamilton Merritt is also American by birth. Why does he disagree with his neighbours?

- Make a quick sketch of Susanna and Maria's bed (pp. 69–70).

- What is a sampler (p. 74)?

- What does Susanna's revenge on Caroline tell you about Susanna (pp. 75–76)?

- In what ways does Tabitha help the Merritt family?

- Why might Hamilton be excited at the prospect of war (p. 84)?

- Describe daily life in the days following the outbreak of war (end of June and beginning of July, 1812). Has it changed? In what ways might this be difficult for Susanna and the women in her family?

- Why is Mr. Seabrook at home (p. 99)?

- When the Merritt men return to the farm on July 28, they have been gone for a month but have not fought at all. What toll has the war already taken on their family and on their farm?

- What is ague (p. 113)? Why would Susanna get it every summer?

- Should Susanna tell someone about Mr. Seabrook's desertion? In what way is Mr. Seabrook a generous man? In what way is he a selfish man?

- When General Brock visits the Merritts, he tells them about the victory at Detroit (p. 126). In what ways did Brock "trick" the Americans in order to win that battle? Why is he angry about the armistice that has been declared?

- Susanna comments that Ellis is odd, that he seems older than he is (p. 131). Do you agree? Why might this be? Write an account of the events of August 26 from Ellis's point of view.

- After reading Susanna's diary entry for September 9 (p. 141), make a Decision Tree to help Tabitha decide if she should marry Samuel and move with him to New York. (Use the reproducible on page 42 if you wish.) What reasons does she have to agree? What reasons does she have to refuse? What do you think she should do?

- Why would Susanna's mother give Mr. Seabrook the money to pay his fine (p. 143)? Why does Susanna describe her as courageous?

- Susanna says that "writing things down is soothing" (p. 146). Do you agree with Susanna? In what ways do you think Susanna's diary is helping her cope with the war?

- As Susanna and her family put away food for winter, Susanna notices that she has finally grown and says that she feels older (p. 152). In what ways has Susanna matured over the past few months? In what ways is she still a child?

- Refer to a map to see how far Mrs. Merritt must travel in order to get to Burlington to be with Caroline.

- Susanna's visit to the dentist (p. 157) is probably not very appealing to modern readers. What other elements of Susanna's life make you happy to be living in the 21st century?

- Why did Ellis want Susanna to come and see General Brock (p. 160)?

- Susanna and Ellis end up in the middle of a battle between Fort George and Fort Niagara. Imagine you are Susanna in the middle of this conflict. What do you see? Hear? Taste? Smell? Feel? What does she mean when she says that she has never felt more alive than at a moment when she may be killed (p. 168)?

- By October 14, Susanna has changed her mind about war being exhilarating. Why?

Brock's ride to Queenston, 1812

- Do you agree with Hamilton that General Brock was reckless (p. 175)?

- Why doesn't Susanna tell Hamilton that she saw General Brock before the Battle of Queenston Heights? Why does she feel guilty?

- Susanna has seen many examples of bravery since the beginning of the diary. Why does she say that Ellis is the bravest boy she has ever met (p. 180)?

- Maria tells Susanna to keep her secret: that she and Charles are betrothed (p. 184). How many secrets is Susanna keeping now?

- Why does Susanna feel older than Abbie (p. 185)?

- Write your version of the conversation Mr. and Mrs. Merritt had upstairs (p. 189).

- Read the Epilogue. Why do you think the diary is titled *Whispers of War*? In what ways are the following two years difficult for the Merritts? Write a diary entry that Susanna might have written in these years.

Extended Activities

- Keep a running list of all the chores that Susanna does in her household. Compare her responsibilities in her household with yours. What kinds of chores does Susanna do? What kinds of chores do you do? Does Susanna contribute to the work of the entire family? To what extent do your chores help the whole family? To what extent are your responsibilities more personal, such as making your own bed?

- Soldiers in wartime are awarded decorations (medals) and citations for bravery. Choose one character in Susanna's diary and design a decoration for her or him. Write a citation explaining what she or he did to earn the award for bravery.

- Have a debate agreeing or disagreeing with the following resolution: Without the help of aboriginal people, the British would have lost Upper Canada to the Americans in the War of 1812.

- Conduct a research project about other wars in which Canadians might have faced divided loyalties. For example, what happened to Ukrainian-Canadians during World War I? Japanese-Canadians in World War II?

- Write a conversation between Mr. Merritt and Mr. Seabrook in which they exchange views about the war. Mr. Merritt should explain why he supports the war; Mr. Seabrook should explain why he opposes it. Use the Writing Dialogue reproducible checklist (p. 24) to assess your work.

- Make a biography poster of one of the important figures of the War of 1812: Isaac Brock, James FitzGibbon, Tecumseh, Laura Secord or John Norton (Teyoninhokarawen). See the reproducible on page 25 for directions.

The meeting of Brock and Tecumseh, 1812

Name ______________________________

Writing Dialogue

Before you write a first draft of the conversation between Mr. Merritt and Mr. Seabrook, brainstorm a list of words you could use instead of "says."

______________ ______________ ______________

______________ ______________ ______________

______________ ______________ ______________

______________ ______________ ______________

After writing a first draft of the dialogue, check your work using the checklist below.

Dialogue Self-Check	Good work!	Okay	Needs attention
Each character clearly states his view on the war.			
Each character gives at least three reasons to support his view.			
The dialogue is appropriate for the speaker.			
The speakers are clearly identified.			
Paragraphs change each time the speaker changes.			
There are quotation marks around the words they speak.			
There are commas between spoken and unspoken words.			

Bibliography Poster

Create a poster that represents a significant person in the War of 1812.

Directions

1. Cut your poster in a shape that represents your person. For example, your poster about General Brock might be cut into the shape of the Brock Monument.

2. Write the person's name on the poster.

3. Place a picture of your person on the poster.

4. Find three other pictures to represent important facts about the person, for example, where they lived or what they accomplished.

5. Using at least three different sources, write down information you locate about the person that will help you complete the following sentences. Include the completed sentences on your poster.

   - Of all the things I did in my life, I am most proud of . . .
   - When I look back on my life, I am sad when I think of . . .
   - If I could have changed one thing about my life, it would have been . . .
   - The person who made the biggest difference in my life was . . . because . . .
   - When people think of me, I hope they say . . .

6. Don't forget to write down the titles and authors of the books or other information sources that you used on the back of your poster.

Whispers of War

The War of 1812 Diary of Susanna Merritt

Bibliography

Non-fiction

Bassett, John. (2004). *Laura Secord.* Toronto: Fitzhenry & Whiteside.

Berton, Pierre. (1991). *Canada Under Siege.* Toronto: McClelland & Stewart.

Berton, Pierre. (1991). *The Death of Isaac Brock.* Toronto: McClelland & Stewart.

Berton, Pierre. (1994). *The Death of Tecumseh.* Toronto: McClelland & Stewart.

Berton, Pierre. (1991). *Revenge of the Tribes.* Toronto: McClelland & Stewart.

Hancock, Pat. (1999). *The Penguin Book of Canadian Biography for Young Readers: Early Canada.* Toronto: Penguin.

Livesey, Robert. (1994). *The Defenders.* Toronto: Stoddart.

Fiction

Crook, Connie Brummel. (1993). *Laura's Choice: The Story of Laura Secord.* Winnipeg: Windflower Communications.

Ibbitson, John. (2000). *Jeremy's War 1812.* Toronto: Kids Can Press.

Lunn, Janet. (2001). *Laura Secord: A Story of Courage.* Toronto: Tundra Books.

Sutherland, Robert. (2000). *A River Apart.* Markham, ON: Fitzhenry & Whiteside.

Trottier, Maxine. (2001). *Under a Shooting Star.* Toronto: Stoddart Kids.

Walters, Eric. (2000). *The Bully Boys.* Toronto: Viking.

Background Information for Teachers

Suthren, Victor. (1999). *The War of 1812.* Toronto: McClelland & Stewart.

Turner, Wesley B. (2000). *The War of 1812: The War that Both Sides Won,* 2nd ed. Toronto: Dundurn Press.

Video

Canada, A People's History, Vol. 5: "A Question of Loyalties, 1775 to 1815." (2000). Toronto: Canadian Broadcasting Corporation.

The War of 1812. (1991). Montreal: National Film Board of Canada.

Websites

http://www.niagara.com/~parkscan/
—Fort George Park website with information for teachers

http://www.pc.gc.ca/lhn-nhs/on/fortgeorge/index_e.asp
—official Parks Canada website for Fort George National Historic Site

A Ribbon of Shining Steel

The Railway Diary of Kate Cameron

Yale, British Columbia, 1882

by Julie Lawson

Summary: In 1882, twelve-year-old Kate Cameron lives in Yale, British Columbia. Her family moved from Ottawa two years before so that her father could work as a bridge foreman on the Canadian Pacific Railway. The work her father does is dangerous, but not as dangerous as the work the thousands of labourers, many of them Chinese, do. Over the next year, Kate provides many details of her life in Yale and outlines the progress of the railway. By August of 1883, after some harrowing adventures, she has been "cut and polished" just like the piece of jade she treasures.

What's Going On in the World in 1882?

- The United States bans Chinese immigrants for ten years.
- Italy, Austria and Germany sign the Triple Alliance.
- Robert Louis Stevenson publishes *Treasure Island*.
- The American Baseball Association is founded.
- Big Bear signs Treaty 6 on behalf of the Plains Cree.
- Oscar Wilde lectures in Ontario, Québec and the Maritimes.
- Circus owner P. T. Barnum buys Jumbo the elephant from the London zoo.

Women's fashion, 1882

Prior Knowledge

Have students view photographs of the terrain around Yale and perhaps create three-dimensional maps in order to appreciate the challenges faced by railway engineers and labourers. Have them consider the financial and human cost of building the railway. Provide background information about those responsible for the planning, financing and building of the railway. What challenges did they face? What dangers did they face? What legacy did they leave for Canada?

Discussion Questions

- Kate's diary begins with her vivid description of a rather frightening adventure. What do we know about her after this first entry? Reread the entry and pay attention to the way she uses capital letters. Why does she do this? What impact does it have on the reader?
- What are "social graces" (p. 6)? Given what we already know about Kate, do you think she has them?
- Trace the Cameron family's route when they moved from Ottawa to Yale (pp. 16–17).
- Draw a sketch map of Yale (pp. 18–20).
- What is Kate's father's job? Why does Kate worry about his safety?
- Complete brief character sketches of all the members of Kate's family.
- Why is it so important to Kate that she have a best friend?
- Why is Anne so hateful to the Chinese workers? Should Kate have responded differently to her?
- Why wouldn't Kate give the jade to the Governor-General?
- Kate enjoys the poem, "The Song of the Locomotive" (pp. 47–48). What makes it so dramatic? Create a "Song of the Automobile" or "Song of the Airplane" in a similar style.

Mules hauling freight wagons, three miles above Yale, early 1880s

- Reread Kate's account of her journey to Aspen Hill Farm (pp. 52–54). What makes Kate an effective writer? Do you think she would be a good journalist? Why or why not?

- Why does Kate enjoy visiting Rachel at Aspen Hill Farm?

- Kate provides a lot of information about her school and her schoolwork. How does her school differ from yours? How is it the same? What do you think the most difficult thing would be about going to school in Yale in the 1880s?

- Why is Anne angry with Kate when she returns from her visit with Rachel? Write Anne's diary entries from November 13 to December 9.

- On December 22, Kate describes the visit of the Public Examiner to her school. Why would children have been tested this way? Why were their results published in the local newspaper? Do you think this is a fair way to evaluate what students have learned? Why or why not?

Stoney Creek Bridge, Selkirk Mountains, ca. 1883

- List all the remedies used to help cure Kate's toothache. What do you think is in "Mrs. Winslow's Soothing Syrup"(p. 84)?

- List all the modes of transportation Kate and her father used to return to Yale from New Westminster. Calculate how long the journey took.

- How do Kate, her brothers and her friends amuse themselves through the winter months?

- Write a short newspaper account of how Kate, Toby and Andrew found the man in the snow (p. 94). Create a story that explains how he came from California and ended up almost frozen in Yale.

- After reading the newspaper clipping about the difficulties of being a woman, think about the differences between Kate's life and the lives of her brothers (p. 101). Are they treated differently? Do they have different responsibilities? Expectations? Why or why not?

- In what way is Mr. Hagan, the editor of the *Sentinel*, courageous? Foolhardy (p. 111)?

- Why is fire such a tremendous hazard in Yale?
- Why does Andrew have to go to Victoria to attend high school (p. 141)?
- The community of Yale has a small picnic on July 1 but quite a large celebration on July 4 (p. 145). Why would this be?
- Why does Mr. Hagan tell Kate the Chinese folk tale (p. 149)? What is the moral of the story?
- After reading Kate's diary entry for the morning of July 29 (p. 157), predict what is going to happen next.
- In your own words, describe how the fire started and spread.
- Anne's mother says that Kate has been a good influence on Anne (p. 167). In what ways has Anne changed Kate?
- After reading Kate's diary entry for August 12, predict what you think will happen when Kate meets Rachel at the college.
- By the end of the diary, in what ways is Kate like the piece of jade she treasures — "cut and polished"?

Canadian Pacific Railway engine, Yale, 1885

CPR poster, 1886

Extended Activities

- Find out more about private girls' colleges in British Columbia like Angela College and St. Ann's Convent, both in Victoria. What subjects did the girls have to take?

- Kate uses some dramatic language and colourful expressions. Record some of your favourites.

- Have a class Victoria Day celebration, like the one Kate describes. Include games such as tug-of-war, sack races, leap-frog races and three-legged races.

- Kate loves poetry. Use her name to write an acrostic poem about her and her life.

- Kate enjoys the sentences her teacher assigns for penmanship: "Rushing rapids rush round rising rivers" or "By being busy, boys become better." These sentences use alliteration. Create your own sentences that use alliteration.

- As you review the diary, make a list of the dangers facing Kate and her community, everything from disease and panthers to the exploding powder works factory. When your list is complete, create a Nineteenth-Century Safety Guide for Newcomers to Yale.

- The Chinese railway workers faced discrimination. Record all the examples that Kate notices. Do some research to find out more about these men, the work they did and the dangers they faced. When you have completed your research, write a tribute to the workers who built the railway, one that might appear on a statue or memorial in the town of Yale.

Chinese section men on handcars, 1886

- Find out more about the politicians and engineers who led the building of the railway, such as Andrew Onderdonk, William Van Horne, and Donald Smith.

- Reread Kate's account of her rescue of Melissa (pp. 158–163). Write a newspaper story for the *Sentinel* that describes what happened. Use the reproducibles on pages 32 and 33 to note the important facts and to organize your writing. Give your story an appropriate headline. Provide an illustration if you wish.

Name ______________________________

Kate's Story — The Facts

Who?	*What?*
Where?	*When?*
Why?	*How?*

News Story Organizer

Many newspaper stories are organized like an inverted triangle, meaning that they start with the most important part of the story — the climax — and then provide the details.

MAIN HEADLINE

SECONDARY HEADLINE

Lead

(Consider beginning with a question, a quotation or a suspenseful statement, to grab the reader's attention.)

Important details

(Provide the facts.)

Less important details

(Include anything else you think is of interest to readers.)

A Ribbon of Shining Steel

The Railway Diary of Kate Cameron

Bibliography

Non-fiction

Berton, Pierre. (1992). *The Railway Pathfinders.* Toronto: McClelland & Stewart.

Berton, Pierre. (1994). *Steel Across the Shield.* Toronto: McClelland & Stewart.

Granfield, Linda. (1993). *Extra! Extra!: The Who, What, Where, When and Why of Newspapers.* Toronto: Kids Can Press.

Hodge, Deborah. (2000). *The Kids Book of Canada's Railway: And How the CPR Was Built.* Toronto: Kids Can Press.

Livesey, Robert. (1997). *The Railways.* Toronto: Stoddart Kids.

Palana, Brett J. (2003). *British Columbia.* San Diego: Thomson Gale.

Fiction

Lawson, Julie. (1993). *White Jade Tiger.* Vancouver: Beach Holme Publishing.

Yee, Paul. (1996). *Ghost Train.* Toronto: Groundwood.

Yee, Paul. (1989). *Tales From Gold Mountain.* Vancouver: Douglas & McIntyre.

Background Information for Teachers

Buck, George H. (1997). *From Summit to Sea: An Illustrated History of Railroads in British Columbia and Alberta.* Calgary: Fifth House.

Cruise, David and Griffiths, Alison. (1988). *Lords of the Line.* Markham, ON: Viking.

Jones, David L. (2002). *Tales of the CPR.* Calgary: Fifth House.

Mitchell, David J. (1995). *All Aboard! The Canadian Rockies by Train.* Vancouver: Douglas & McIntyre.

Turner, Robert D. (1987). *West of the Great Divide: An Illustrated History of the Canadian Pacific Railway in British Columbia, 1880-1986.* Victoria: Sono Nis Press.

Websites

http://www.bcarchives.gov.bc.ca/index.htm
—the Royal BC Museum, BC Archives has a wonderful collection of visual records related to Yale and area

http://www.cprheritage.com/index.htm
—the official site of the Canadian Pacific Railway Archives

http://www.library.ubc.ca/chung/intro.html
—the Chung Collections at the University of British Columbia, with information about the Chinese experience in Canada and the building of the CPR

http://www.heritage.gov.bc.ca/yale/yale.htm
—British Columbia heritage site on historic Yale

http://www.bcarchives.gov.bc.ca/exhibits/timemach/galler08/frames/index.htm
—British Columbia Archives on history of transportation, with links to information about the Canadian Pacific Railway

Brothers Far from Home

The World War I Diary of Eliza Bates

Uxbridge, Ontario, 1916

by Jean Little

Summary: Twelve-year-old Eliza Bates is the daughter of a Presbyterian minister. As the diary opens at Christmas, 1916, she is angry with her sister Verity who treats her like a young child and she is obviously missing her eldest brother Hugo, who is serving with the Canadian forces overseas. Another brother, Jack, and his friend Rufus are celebrating their last Christmas with the family before they, too, go overseas. Over the course of the diary, which covers the next two years, Eliza matures. She records the difficulties of life on the home front during the war and befriends a neighbour who returns from the war a victim of shell shock. In April, 1917, the Bates family receives a telegram with news they were dreading: Hugo has been killed at the Battle of Vimy Ridge. As the family members cope with their grief, they hear that Jack has been wounded. By the time the diary ends at Christmas, 1918, each family member has been changed by his or her experience of the war.

What's Going On in the World in 1916?

- Prohibition comes into effect in Ontario.
- James Joyce publishes *Portrait of the Artist as a Young Man*.
- Daylight Saving Time is introduced in Britain.
- Jazz sweeps the United States.
- The Professional Golfers' Association (PGA) of America is formed.
- Manitoba, Saskatchewan and Alberta women win the right to vote in provincial elections.
- The first birth control clinic opens in the United States.
- A fire destroys the Centre Block of the Parliament Buildings in Ottawa.

Prior Knowledge

Provide students with some background information about the causes and conduct of World War I. Explain Canada's involvement and the toll the war took on the civilian population as well as on the men of the armed forces. The diary addresses the theme of social changes that were a result of the war, such as the greater social and economic opportunities for women, so some attention should be given to an exploration of this as well.

Discussion Questions

- The real author of this diary, Jean Little, is particularly adept at capturing the language of this historical period. Keep a running list of the vocabulary or expressions that are unfamiliar to you — or are of particular interest — and their meanings. Eliza's first entry might result in such examples as: manse, limpet, changeling, good scout, gall, pudding face or lame ducks.
- After reading Eliza's Christmas entries, make a quick draft of her family tree and brainstorm a list of the things you already know about characters like Eliza (for example, she likes to read), Verity, Mother, Father and Grandmother.
- After reading Eliza's Boxing Day entry, correct and make additions to the family tree you sketched earlier. Also correct or add any information you learned about Eliza's family members. Continue to add to your character sketches as you read on through the diary.
- Why do you think Eliza is particularly fond of Hugo?
- Do you think it's true that people notice your weak moments and never your strong ones (p. 22)? Write a journal entry about one of your strong moments you wish someone had noticed.
- Based on the information Eliza has provided about Jack and Norah (pp. 24–26), do you think Norah is as fond of Jack as he seems to be of her?
- Why would Eliza's father frown on dancing and playing cards on Sundays?
- Eliza is quite an effective writer. Note her use of the phrase: "Charlie springs away like an antelope" (p. 25). What is the term for the literary device Eliza uses here? Why is this effective? Review her previous diary entries and see if you can find other examples of these devices.

- After reading Eliza's entry for New Year's Day, 1917, identify the clues that indicate her family's Scottish heritage.

- Eliza describes seeing the boys off to war. Discuss how other characters would feel at that moment and then write a journal entry about this event from the point of view of some other character: Jack, Mother, Father or Norah for example.

- Eliza writes about the Wesley family (p. 30). She is referring to the family of John and Charles Wesley, the founders of the Methodist movement within the Church of England in the eighteenth century. Find out more about these brothers and sing some of Charles's hymns, the most famous of which Eliza mentions. Why do you think Eliza's family might find these hymns so appealing? Why was hymn-singing an important part of their family life?

The 8th Battalion "Little Black Devils" going into the line, October 1917

- Eliza mentions that when she was little, she was afraid of the dark (p. 32). How did she overcome her fear? What does this tell you about her brother Hugo?

- Do you agree with Eliza that Verity is "stuffy and proper" (p. 35)? Why or why not? Write Verity's diary entry for the evening of January 3, in order to consider her point of view.

- Why do you think Eliza dislikes being a "preacher's kid"? What unique pressures do you think she might face as a result?

- Mr. Royle was given a white feather to embarrass him into joining up to fight, but Eliza imagines that perhaps his eyesight prevents him from enlisting (pp. 37–38). Find out what kinds of health issues might have prevented men from volunteering for the armed services during that time.

- What resolutions does Eliza make for the new year (p. 39)?

- What is the matter with Cornelia Webb? Why is Eliza so concerned that the girls in her class call her and Cornelia "birds of a feather"(p. 46)?

- Why would Dr. Webb reject Eliza's father and insist that there is no God (p. 48)?

- Eliza's father is angry with her brother Charlie for saying that the Germans roasted babies (p. 52). Why do you think such stories were common during the war?

- Listen to "Onward Christian Soldiers." Do you agree with Eliza that it is stirring and sad at the same time? Why do you think she has such conflicting feelings about the war?

Wounded Canadians on the way to an aid post.
Battle of Passchendaele, November 1917

- What is the difference between a bathroom and a privy (p. 54)?

- What do you think Eliza means when she calls Mrs. Webb a "brick"?

- How is Eliza going to help the war effort?

- What does Eliza mean when she says the dog is full of "true grit"(p. 58)? In what way are Belle and Sam also full of true grit?

- Why is the dog named Isaac? Do you have any pets with special names?

- Richard Webb comes home because he has shell shock. What do you think that means? Predict what kinds of symptoms he might have.

- Why would Dr. Webb disapprove of women working outside the home (p. 64)?

- Do you think Eliza would be a good teacher? Why or why not?

- After reading Eliza's description of Richard Webb (pp. 66–67), what do you think shell shock means? Read a definition and description of shell shock in a non-fiction book and decide if the author has given an accurate description of its effects.

- Eliza's mother tells her that the Webb family has had "more than its share of troubles" (p. 71). Summarize the troubles facing the family. Identify ways the Bates family is trying to help.

- What was Richard going to do when Eliza found him? How did she reach out to him? Why doesn't she tell the Webbs what happened?

- Why do you think Eliza and Verity get on better than they used to (p. 83)? What other examples are there in the diary of the war bringing people closer together?

- How do the members of Eliza's family support each other when they hear about Hugo's death?

- Eliza discovers that Hugo may have been shot by a Canadian for disobeying orders. Military discipline did indeed mean that soldiers were shot in the heat of battle if they disobeyed direct orders. As tragic as the consequences are in the case of Eliza's family, can you think of any reasons why such strict military discipline might have been necessary?

Sir Douglas Haig congratulating Canadians. Battle of Amiens, August 1918

- Why are Eliza and her younger siblings sent to Aunt Martha's (p. 104)? Look on a map to see the distance between Uxbridge and Guelph. Why would the children have to change trains in Toronto?

- Why would Aunt Martha call her red hat her "small rebellion hat" (p. 113)?

- What does Aunt Martha mean by the term "modern woman" (p. 116)? In what ways is Eliza already prepared to be such a woman?

- In some ways is life easier for Aunt Martha and Grandmother in Guelph than for the Bates family in Uxbridge? What kinds of things do they have that people in larger towns and cities did not have during the war?

- Eliza mentions that Verity is getting big and official-looking envelopes in the mail (p. 124). What do you think she is up to?

- Why does Rufus's commanding officer disapprove of wartime marriages (p. 135)?

- Eliza finally discovers what Verity was up to (p. 136). Check your prediction — were you correct? Why was Verity so secretive about her plans?

- When Verity recounts her adventures in nursing school, Eliza is amazed (pp. 141–143). In what ways has Verity changed since the beginning of the diary? Why might she have changed?

- What happens to Jack?
- In what way is Eliza deceiving her parents (p. 152)?
- What kind of help do you think Rosemary needs (p. 156)? How do you think Jack is going to help her?
- In her entry for Friday, December 7, Eliza talks about the explosion in Halifax harbour. Find out more about this tragic event.
- Eliza receives elocution lessons from her parents for her birthday. What are these? Why would people take lessons to learn how to speak?
- After reading Eliza's diary entry for Christmas, 1917, review how her life has changed in the past year. How has she changed? Why?
- On Friday, April 12, Eliza writes that something exciting is bound to happen (p. 166). Predict what the next entry will be about.
- Why won't Jack tell his parents about his marriage and his son?
- Eliza says that perhaps Jack has scars inside as well as outside. What kinds of scars does he bear?
- What does Aunt Martha's telegram mean (p. 177)?
- Does Eliza do the right thing in telling her mother Jack's secrets? Why or why not?
- Do you agree with Aunt Martha that Eliza has imagination and empathy (p. 184)? What examples of these qualities can you find from the diary?
- Eliza mentions the impact on Uxbridge of the Spanish influenza. Find out more about this epidemic and the impact it had worldwide. Do we face anything like this today?
- What does Eliza mean when she says that, for them, the war will never be over (p. 194)?
- Who does Eliza's "Dear Reader" turn out to be?
- Why was the epitaph that Eliza chose for her mother appropriate (p. 202)? Write an epitaph for another character in the diary and explain why it is appropriate.

Extended Activities

- Pretend you are Eliza on April 12, 1918. Write a letter to an advice columnist asking if you should tell your parents about Jack's marriage and child. Complete the Decision Tree reproducible (p. 42) to help you organize your thoughts for the letter to the columnist. Use the Plan Your Paragraph reproducible (p. 43) to organize your arguments and then write the advice columnist's response to Eliza.

- As you read the diary, keep a list of all the ways the war has an impact on the daily life of the Bates family. When you complete the list, choose what you think would have been the most difficult thing about life on the home front during World War I. Defend your answer.

- Review the information you have about Hugo by the end of the diary. Write a eulogy celebrating his life.

- How would the story change if Hugo had come home safely? Write Eliza's diary entry about the day Hugo came home.

- Visit the World War I memorial(s) in your community. Contact your local archives or museum to find out more about the men on the memorial and about others in your community who served overseas during World War I. Look up their attestation papers and enlistment forms on the National Archives database. Read a local history to find out more about life in your community during the war.

- Plan a fundraiser for a global cause like the one Eliza participated in to raise money for the war effort. Encourage participants to memorize and recite poetry, play music or present a tableau.

- Complete a research project on the battle of Vimy Ridge, the battle in which Eliza's brother Hugo was killed. Why was this such an important battle for Canadians? The territory of Vimy Ridge was given to Canada by the people of France to thank them for the efforts of the Canadian Expeditionary Force in this battle. It is the site of an important Canadian war memorial. Find out more about the memorial and its continued significance for Canadians.

Five thousand Canadians leaving Southampton on the SS *Olympia*, April 16, 1919

Name ____________________

Decision Tree

The problem:

One solution:

Another solution:

Consequences:

Consequences:

The best solution is:

Name ______________________________

Plan Your Paragraph

Your position: ______________________________

____

____

____

____

Reason A	Reason B	Reason C
____________	____________	____________
____________	____________	____________
____________	____________	____________
____________	____________	____________
____________	____________	____________

On the other hand . . . ______________________________

____

____

But I still say . . . ______________________________

____

____

Your conclusion: ______________________________

____

____

____

____

Brothers Far from Home
The World War I Diary of Eliza Bates

Bibliography

Non-fiction
Adams, Simon. (2001). *World War I.* New York: Dorling Kindersley.
Granfield, Linda. (1995). *In Flanders Fields: The Story of the Poem by John McCrae.* Toronto: Stoddart Kids.
Granfield, Linda. (2002). *Where Poppies Grow: A World War I Companion.* Toronto: Stoddart Kids.
Hatt, Christine. (2000). *World War I, 1914–1918.* London: Evans.
Morton, Desmond. (1983). *Years of Conflict, 1911–1921.* Toronto: Grolier.
Morton, Desmond. (1986). *Album of the Great War.* Toronto: Grolier.

Fiction
Debon, Nicholas. (2002). *A Brave Soldier.* Toronto: Douglas & McIntyre.
Haworth-Attard, Barbara. (2001). *Flying Geese.* Toronto: Harper Collins.
McKay, Sharon E. (2000). *Charlie Wilcox.* Toronto: Stoddart Kids. See also *Charlie Wilcox's Great War* (2003).
Morpurgo, Michael. (2003). *Private Peaceful.* London: Collins.
Wilson, John A. (2003). *And in the Morning.* Toronto: Kids Can Press.

Background Information for Teachers
Bashow, David. (2000). *Knights of the Air: Canadian Fighter Pilots in the First World War.* Toronto: McArthur & Co.
Berton, Pierre. (1986). *Vimy.* Toronto: McClelland and Stewart.
Freeman, Bill. (1999). *Far From Home: Canadians in the First World War.* Toronto: McGraw-Hill Ryerson.
Gwyn, Sandra. (1992). *Tapestry of War: A Private View of Canadians in the Great War.* Toronto: HarperCollins.
Morton, Desmond and Granatstein, J.L. (1989). *Marching to Armageddon.* Toronto: Lester & Orpen Dennys.
Morton, Desmond. (1993). *When Your Number's Up: The Canadian Soldier in the First World War.* Toronto: Random House of Canada.

Video
Far From Home: Canada and the Great War. (1999). Norflicks Production/Morningstar Entertainment.
John McCrae's War: In Flanders Fields. (1998). National Film Board of Canada.
World War One: Canada's Role (1992). Classroom Video.

Websites
http://www.collectionscanada.ca/02/02010601_e.html
—National Archives of Canada database of soldiers of the Canadian Expeditionary Force

http://collections.ic.gc.ca/turner/
—Jack Turner's War

http://www.cbc.ca/news/vimy/
—CBC News backgrounder on Vimy

Name ____

Turning Points

As the diary progresses, the fictional author changes.
On the organizer below, describe the author's character at the beginning of the diary and at the end. Then identify the points in the diary when she changes. Give the page number of the turning points and brief explanations for them.

Character at the beginning ____________________________

Turning point 1 ____________________________

Turning point 2 ____________________________

Character at the end ____________________________

Creating a Tableau

A tableau (full name: tableau vivant*) is a living picture. A group of students can arrange themselves in a silent and motionless scene to represent a moment in a Dear Canada diary. Tableaux help develop understanding and response to literature, and require good group or collaborative skills.*

Preparation

- How do we express our feelings or attitudes through our bodies? Try modelling what a sad person looks like, as well as a happy person, an angry person and a frightened person.

- Practise tableaux in pairs. Create some situations or scenarios. (Some examples might be a father and son playing catch, a mother feeding her child, two children arguing over a toy.) Pose in one of the scenes you have invented. Remember that you cannot speak or move! Present your tableau to the class. Have the other students in the class guess the scene you are posing.

- After sharing several scenes, consider which tableaux were most effective. How did the students convey emotion through their bodies and expressions?

Procedure

- In a group of two to five, create a tableau for a critical moment in the diary. In addition to conveying the emotion of the moment, it is important to create a visually interesting scene. For example, you could set yourselves up to create different levels in height and an interesting placement on the floor. You may even use props if you wish.

- Prior to presenting your tableau to the class, write a paragraph together identifying the scene you are presenting and the characters involved, and explaining why your group felt this was a critical moment in the diary.

- Present your tableau. Once you are frozen in your scenes, your teacher will tap each of you on the shoulder one at a time. This tap is your signal to break your silence and recite a short monologue describing your character's situation and feelings.

Writing a Review of a Dear Canada Diary

You have been asked to write a review of a Dear Canada diary for the magazine, *Canadian History Today*. Your task is not only to discuss whether the diary is good literature, you also need to comment on its value as history. Make sure you answer the following questions:

- Who is the real author of the diary? What other books has she written?
- Does the author have a personal or family connection to this story or this event in history? If so, what is it? Do you think such a connection would make it easier or more difficult to write about the event?
- What important event in Canadian history is featured in this story? Why is this event worth writing a book about? What kinds of things does the diary tell us about that are often missing from non-fiction history books?
- After reading about the life of a fictional girl in this period of history, do you think life was better or worse then? Defend your answer.
- In what ways has life stayed the same?
- Do you think the author of the diary has presented a "realistic" sense of what life was like then? How?
- If you could travel to that time, what do you think would be the most difficult thing about living then? What would be the best thing?
- What makes the fictional author of the diary seem real? Is she someone you would like to get to know?
- What questions do you have for the real author of the diary? What questions do you have about the time or event in Canadian history portrayed in the diary?

Photo Credits

Page 9: Joslyn Art Museum, Omaha, Nebraska, William Adolphe Bougeureau, *The Knitting Girl (La Tricoteuse)*, detail, JAM. 1931.106.

Page 11: National Archives of Canada, Arthur E. Elias, *Landing of the Girls Sent Out as Brides in 1667 at Quebec*, C-029486.

Pages 12 and 13: C.W. Jefferys, *First Convent of the Ursuline Nuns* and *Mohawk Indians in Front of an Elm Bark Lodge*, reproduced with permission of the C.W. Jefferys Estate Archive.

Page 14: National Archives of Canada, Charles Louis Simonneau, *Soeur Marguerite Bourgeois*, C-008986.

Page 18: Art Renewal Center: artrenewal.org, William Adolphe Bougeureau, *The Little Knitter*, detail.

Page 20 (upper): Archives of Ontario, George Theodore Berthon, *Major-General Sir Isaac Brock, K. B.*, 694158.

Page 20 (lower): National Archives of Canada, Francis Hall, *View from Queenston Heights, Upper Canada (Queenston, Ont.), 1816/1817*, C-003240.

Pages 22 and 23: C.W. Jefferys, *Brock's Ride to Queenston, 1812* and *Meeting of Brock and Tecumseh, 1812*, reproduced with permission of the C.W. Jefferys Estate Archive.

Page 27 (upper): Aberdeen Art Gallery Museums, John Everett Millais, *Bright Eyes*, detail, 1877.

Page 27 (lower): C.W. Jefferys, *Fashions of the Eighties, 1882*, reproduced with permission of the C.W. Jefferys Estate Archive.

Pages 28 and 29: Glenbow Archives, Calgary, Canada, *Mules hauling freight wagons on Cariboo Road, Fountain Bluff, British Columbia*, NA-3232-54 and *Stoney Creek Bridge, Selkirk Mountains, British Columbia*, PA-3544-2a.

Page 30 (left): Glenbow Archives, Calgary, Canada, *Canadian Pacific Railway engine, Yale, British Columbia*, NA-2269-1.

Page 30 (right): Canadian Pacific Railway Archives, A.20718.

Page 31: Glenbow Archives, Calgary, Canada, *Chinese section men on handcars, Canadian Pacific Railway*, NA-387-27.

Page 35: Dalhousie University Archives, Waldren Studios Collection, Box 54, File 103, *Miss McLean*, 1904 detail.

Pages 37, 38, 39 and 41: National Archives of Canada, Department of National Defence, *The 8th Bn. "Little Black Devils" going into the line, wearing respirators at the alert, October, 1917*, PA-001994; *Wounded Canadians on way to aid-post, Battle of Passchendaele, November, 1917*, PA-002107; *Sir Douglas Haig congratulating Canadians, Battle of Amiens, August, 1918*, PA-002900; and *5000 Canadians leaving Southampton on SS* Olympia *on April 16th, 1919*, PA-006049.

National Library of Canada Cataloguing in Publication

Von Heyking, Amy J. (Amy Jeanette), 1965-
Teaching with Dear Canada books / Amy von Heyking.

Includes bibliographical references.
ISBN 0-7791-1385-3 (v. 1).—ISBN 0-439-96974-3 (v. 2)

1. Children's stories, Canadian (English)—Study and teaching (Elementary) 2. Canada—History—Study and teaching (Elementary) 3. Social sciences—Study and teaching (Elementary)—Canada. 4. English language—Study and teaching (Elementary) 5. Language arts (Elementary) I. Title.

PS8039.F5V65 2002 C813'.54 C2002-901144-2

6 5 4 3 2 1 Printed in Canada 04 05 06 07 08